Why Love a Puffin?

by Roger L. Stevens, Jr.

First Edition

Published by Maine Focus Photography
P.O. Box 398
Lincoln, Maine 04457

If you have any questions or comments about this book, you can contact Roger L. Stevens, Jr. at
Maine Focus Photography
P.O. Box 398
Lincoln, Maine 04457
1-877-794-1928
mefocus@myfairpoint.net
www.mainefocusphotography.biz

Proudly manufactured in the U.S.A. by:
J.S. McCarthy Printers
15 Darin Drive
Augusta, Maine 04330

ISBN 978-1-5323-7457-9
For information about custom editions, special sales, and wholesale orders, please contact Maine Focus Photography.

The Atlantic Puffin is the iconic symbol of the Gulf of Maine. Its bright beak and orange feet make it quite distinct from other seabirds in the area. Puffins are a pelagic bird, which means they spend very little time on land, preferring to bob up and down in the ocean. The only time that mature puffins will spend time on land is from early June until August, just giving it time to breed, prepare a burrow, and to hatch their baby chicks called pufflings. Puffin burrows are dug into dirt or hidden among rock caves to ensure that the chicks are safe from predators such as gulls. During this time, the parents continuously fly offshore, sometimes diving to depths of nearly 200 feet to catch fish and shrimp to feed their hungry offspring.

Many visitors come each year to visit these "Parrots of the Sea", with some being fortunate as to land on the islands that the puffins call home for a few months. These photos were taken on one of these islands. If you wish to take a tour to Machias Seal Island you can visit either boldcoast.com or seawatchtours.com.

I hope you enjoy this book as much as I enjoyed spending time with its subjects!

Sincerely,

Roger L. Stevens, Jr.

"Why love a puffin?",

some people inquire.

We love them because of

their clown-like attire,

their soft, fluffy feathers,

their colorful beaks,

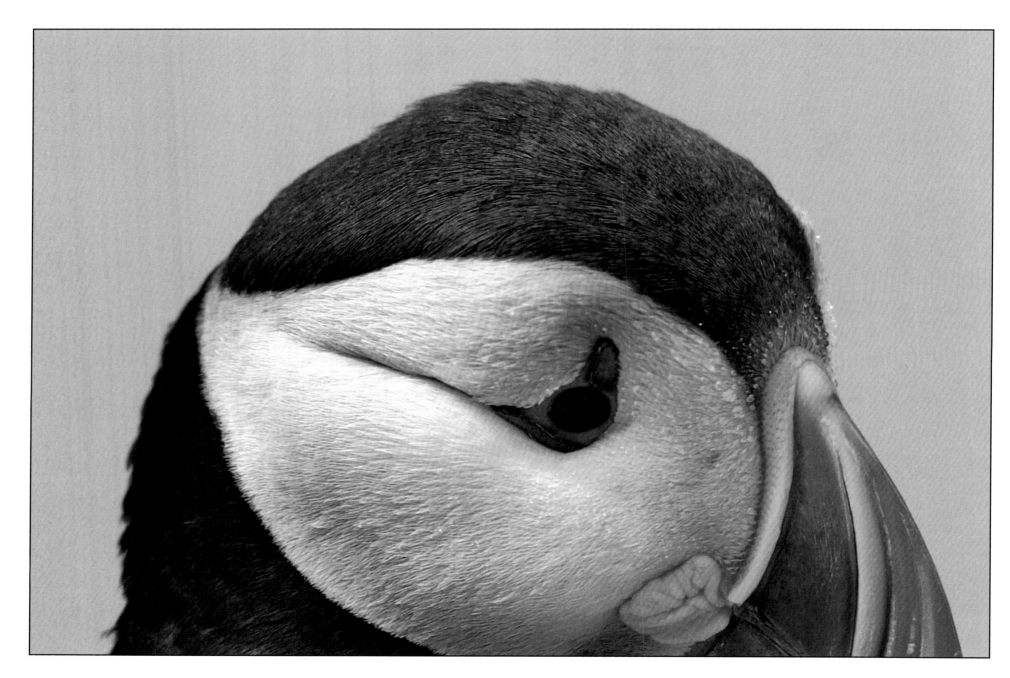

their sweet, soulful eyes

and round chubby cheeks.

It's because they share kisses

with sisters and brothers;

they make really nice neighbors,

and they fly well with others!

We love that they live

by lighthouses and flowers,

that they stare out to sea

for hours and hours . . .

We love that they also

like living on ledges.

We think that they're cute

peeking over the edges.

We love how they look

when they're having a rest

while their mate takes a watch

guarding pufflings and nest.

We love they take turns

flying out to the sea

to bring back a meal

for the puffin baby.

We love when they preen

and spread their wee wings.

We love when they yawn

and do silly things!

So why we love puffins

should be crystal clear;

what's NOT to love

'bout a bird that's so dear?!

This book is dedicated to Captain Andrew "Andy" Patterson, owner and operator of the "Barbara Frost". Captain Andy has been running Puffin Tours out of his home port in Cutler, Maine for over 30 years. He, along with Captain Peter Wilcox out of Grand Manan, Canada, are the only two charter Captains who are allowed the privilege to land 14 customers each per day on Machias Seal Island, where these photos were taken.

I met Captain Andy some 16 years ago on my first such journey to this rugged, yet beautiful island, and we have been friends since. His knowledge of the sea, the creatures that live there and his genuine good nature make it a pleasure for anyone lucky enough to sail on the "Barbara Frost".

Thank you, Andy, for safely making the passage to Machias Seal Island and helping us discover its wonders.